Limiting Beliefs

RUTH LOGAN

CONTENTS

.

INTRODUCTION

How many times a day do you say to yourself that you can't do something? It may range from "quite a few" and "all the time." The doubt will not leave until you start examining the way you think and change it. That negativity holds you back and until you believe you are able to change it, it won't happen.

Sometimes we use words like "I mustn't" or "I shouldn't" which we use to protect ourselves. For example, in a trying situation at work you might say to yourself, "I mustn't lose my temper." In this example, the words "I mustn't" are a reminder to yourself of a standard you have set for yourself or of a rule that applies in a given situation.

However, there are other times when we say these words and they limit us. That hold us back from living up to our true potential. Here are some examples:

- I can't learn how to dance, I have two left feet!
- I won't even bother to try losing weight, there's no point.
- I mustn't disobey that rule, even though I think it is a bad rule.
- I am not good enough for this job.

What do all of these statements have in common? They are limiting beliefs, and my goal with this book is to share with you the things I learned – things that helped me get rid of my limiting beliefs for good.

What Is a Limiting Belief?

A limiting belief is something that we believe to be true – as opposed to something we know to be true. Things we know are facts, such as "My eyes are blue," or "I know how to ride a bicycle." Limiting beliefs are about your perception of yourself, who you are as a person and what you are capable of accomplishing.

We acquire our limiting beliefs over a lifetime. Some limiting beliefs may come to us from our parents. If your mother told you at a young age that you would never be an Olympic athlete, for example, you might accept her statement and internalize it. In other words, you would start to believe that it was true that you could never accomplish that goal. Because you believed it, you would probably not put the same effort into it that you would if you did believe you could do it.

Other limiting beliefs may take root because you try something once, and things don't go well. It's sometimes tempting to give up, to not put in the work that a task requires because you fear that you will fail.

It is when you give up easily that limiting beliefs are the most dangerous. You have probably heard it said that human beings use only a small portion of their brains. That is true – and it is just as true that when you let limiting beliefs govern your life, you are using only a tiny fraction of your potential.

Psychological Impact of Limiting Beliefs

You might be wondering why you need to be worried about limiting beliefs. Are they truly hurting you? For the most part, the answer is yes. There are certainly some limiting beliefs that are protective. For example, it is essential that you believe that you cannot fly, because it is objectively true that you cannot. If you stopped believing that you can't do it, you could hurt yourself.

The other type of limiting belief, though, is the kind that can do serious damage to your self-esteem. Whether a limiting belief is the result of personal experience, education, or some type of faulty logic, the result is the same.

Limiting beliefs can make you feel that you are unable to extricate yourself from a bad situation, such as a toxic work environment or an unhappy relationship. They can prevent you from trying new things, from learning new things, and from getting on with your life.

One of the most insidious things about limiting beliefs is that they operate on a subconscious level. You might not even be aware of the ways in which your personal beliefs about who you are and what you can do are holding you back. I certainly wasn't. Deeply-held limiting beliefs can influence our behavior in ways we don't realize, and can result in things like passive aggressive behavior and self-sabotage.

All of us, at some point, have said to ourselves, "I don't know why I just did that." The people around us might hear that and think we're not being honest, but it's true – we don't know. Chances are good that the reason, the real reason, is that we have a limiting belief that pushed us to do something that was detrimental to our well-being.

Solutions

Now that you understand what limiting beliefs are, let's talk about how you can get rid of them. I had a whole slew of limiting beliefs that were holding me back. I had a job that I hated, and I was in an unhappy relationship, too. The exercises I'm going to share with you are things that I did to help me snap out of it and make my life what I wanted it to be. If you're willing to take the steps outlined in this book, you can do the same thing. You can have the life you want, and it's only going to take a week for you to permanently change your way of thinking. Each day, I'll tell you about a different aspect of limiting beliefs, and I'll give you an easy and practical exercise that will help you figure out the things that are holding you back.

We'll start by digging a bit deeper in terms of understanding the different kinds of limiting beliefs so that you can identify yours. Then we'll identify your goals, and talk about how you can change your internal monologue to help keep those limiting beliefs at bay.

Later in the week, you'll learn how to eliminate excuses, and raise the standards you have for yourself. We'll also talk about how to turn your new beliefs into actions. By the end of the week, you will be able to see a dramatic change in both the way you think, and the way you feel.

Let's get started.

DAY 1 – WHAT ARE YOUR LIMITING BELIEFS?

The first step in overcoming your limiting beliefs is to know what they are. As I stated in the introduction, many of us have limiting beliefs that act on us on a subconscious level. What that means, of course, is that you are not consciously aware of them – and you need to be able to identify your limiting beliefs in order to eliminate them. When I started digging, I found all kinds of limiting beliefs that I didn't know I had.

To help you get at the root of the limiting beliefs that are holding you back, let's take a closer look at the different ways we can come to hold limiting beliefs.

1.   **Experience** – We all have experiences in our lives that can have a profound impact on the way we see ourselves. A young child who gets lost in a park may go through life believing that all parks are dangerous, or that he cannot trust himself to find his way.

2.   **Education** – As children, we look up to our parents and teachers, and we tend to believe the things they tell us are true. That can be a great thing when it comes to learning the multiplication tables, but it's not so great in some cases. If a teacher tells a child that she's not good at math, that child may internalize her statement and start to believe that it's true. She might not work as hard in math class and simply resign herself to mediocre grades, when in reality, she might be able to do very well if she put in the effort.

3.   **Fear** – While human beings are more evolved than most animals on the planet, we still have a deeply-rooted animal instinct that helps to protect us. However, sometimes our fears can be severely limiting. For example, you might have a vacation planned, and the week before, you see a news report about a plane crash. The chance of any particular plane crashing is incredibly small, but a fearful person might cancel the vacation

because she fears a crash.

4.   **Faulty logic** – Some of the most dangerous limiting beliefs are the result of faulty logic. You might take a tiny bit of information, and extrapolate it into something that you see as an iron-clad generalization.

Now that you have a better idea of where limiting beliefs come from let's go into more detail about the different kinds of limiting beliefs. This information is going to help you with the first day's exercise, identifying your limiting beliefs. Let's look at each limiting belief as if it were a statement you make to yourself.

1.   **I am/I am not.** Perhaps the most dangerous type of limiting belief is this one because, as a rule, people don't believe they can change who they are. If a teacher gets frustrated with a student and says, "You're just not intelligent," those words can root themselves deep in the child's psyche. She comes to believe them, and the belief that she is not intelligent may keep her from attempting to learn new things, or from studying for tests, or even from applying to colleges. Other examples might include narrower definitions of self, such as "I'm an actuary, I am not an artist," or "I'm not athletic."

2.   **I can't.** Another very common form of limiting belief is the "I can't" statement. You probably say this kind of thing internally – or even out loud – more than you realize. The person who says, "I can't fly a plane" will never go to flight school. The person who says, "I can't handle disappointment" won't be able to handle disappointment.

3.   **I must/I mustn't.** Limiting beliefs that begin with the words "I must" or "I mustn't" can sometimes be helpful. They have their roots in cultural norms and ethics. However, at times you need to push past them. For example, societal norms told Rosa Parks that she needed to give up her seat on the bus, and probably on most days she would have done exactly that. One day she decided to ignore her limiting belief, the one imposed on her by society – and by doing so, she changed the world

4. **I do/I don't.** You probably know someone who limits himself by using statements about what he does and doesn't do. Limiting beliefs like this can range from the mundane (I don't like sushi, from the person who's never tried it) to the monumental (I don't deserve to be happy).

5. **Other people do/don't.** Not all limiting beliefs are self-contained. At one time or another, you have compared yourself unfavorably to another person. Limiting beliefs that have their roots in the behavior of other people might include things like, "Jane is a much better artist than I am, so I should just leave that to her." You might also get caught up in worrying about what other people will think. For example, "People will think I'm frivolous if I spend my time doing this".

6. **That's just the way things are.** The final kind of limiting belief has to do with the way we see the world at large. Rather than looking at our limitations, or comparing ourselves to others, we tell ourselves, "Well, I can't do that because it's just the way the world works." What's important to remember about this kind of belief is that every single great invention or discovery started because someone was willing to say, "I see the world in a different way." If scientists didn't have the ability to look beyond the way things are, we wouldn't have things like the polio vaccine or the Hubble Space Telescope.

Self-Talk Exercise

Now that you have a clear understanding of what limiting beliefs are, and what they might sound like, let's talk about your first exercise. Today, your assignment is to pay close attention to your self-talk. Self-talk is the internal dialogue you have with yourself, all day long, every day. It is in this self-talk that limiting beliefs make themselves known. Reading this, you may already have some ideas about your limiting beliefs. Write them down, but still pay attention to your thoughts during the day. Notice the times when you resist doing something – when you try to talk yourself out of something, or when you're feeling bad about yourself. Pay attention to the way you react to other people, and to the attributes you assign to yourself in comparison to them. Write everything down, even if it seems inconsequential.

At the end of the day, you may be surprised to see how many limiting beliefs you have. I was amazed at how negative my internal thoughts were. I had just accepted those limiting thoughts as if I had no way to change them. Don't worry about the negativity of your thoughts – just remember, by the end of the week, you'll be rid of them.

DAY 2 – GOAL SETTING

Welcome to day two. Before we get started, I want you to read over your list of limiting beliefs from yesterday. Carry them with you today, because you are going to need them.

Identifying your limiting beliefs is the first step toward getting rid of them. The list you hold in your hand is your road map – a guide that will help you achieve more in your life than you ever thought was possible. Life achievements and goals are the subjects of today's lesson, so with that in mind, let's talk a little bit about the importance of setting goals.

Why You Need Goals

Chances are good you already have some goals in life. Maybe you want to get a promotion at work, lose ten pounds, or travel to Singapore. Having goals is important for many reasons, but sometimes your limiting beliefs can affect the things you see as goals.

What does having goals do for us?

1. It gives us something to strive for. Without concrete goals, many people can get bogged down and stop moving forward with their lives. When you are working toward something, it keeps you motivated and energetic.

2. It tells you what you really want. A lot of times, you might feel unsure about what you desire from life. When you set a goal for yourself, though, it serves as a reminder of what is important to you – what you value.

3. It keeps you accountable for mistakes and failures. We all make mistakes, but that can be a good thing if we are willing to learn from them. Goals help keep you on track – when you have a clear goal, you can hold yourself accountable for things you do wrong and take steps to correct your errors.

4.   It makes big tasks seem achievable. Sometimes you might have a really big goal, one that seems impossible. When you break a large goal down into smaller goals, those smaller steps can seem easier to take than they would if you just focused on the long-term goal.

5.   It makes it easier for you to believe in yourself. When you set goals for yourself, you are telling yourself that you think you can achieve them. The belief that you can do something often has a huge effect on whether or not you will do it.

Having goals is necessary if you want to grow as a person. If you have nothing to strive for, you may find yourself simply going through the motions in life like I was. When your life becomes stagnant, the stagnation can spread. You can start to think that you can never change anything, and that is especially damaging.

How Limiting Beliefs Affect Your Goals

Today's exercise is about setting goals, as you may have guessed. Before we talk about what you need to do, let's first take a moment to discuss the way the limiting beliefs you identified yesterday might be affecting the goals you set for yourself.

Let's look at a common goal as an example. Many people want to lose a few pounds, and they have goals for losing weight, eating healthier, and exercising more. Their goals might be modest (I want to lose ten pounds before my high school reunion) or ambitious (I am severely overweight, and I need to lose a hundred pounds for my health.) I guarantee, though, that the people who are successful at losing weight are the ones who believe they can do it.

Instead of saying "I can't lose weight," they are saying, "I can lose weight."

Instead of saying "I am fat," they are saying, "I am carrying some extra weight now, but it doesn't have to be that way."

Instead of saying "Other people lose weight easily, but I don't," they are saying, "If other people can do it, I can too!"

Do you see the difference? When you move beyond your limiting beliefs and eliminate them from your goal-setting process, you make it much more likely that you will shoot for the stars – and reach them.

Goal Setting Exercise

You need goals, and today's exercise is going to help you set some new goals for yourself, without being shackled by your limiting beliefs.

To start, write down a list of your current goals. When you look at those goals, do you see any ways in which your limiting beliefs are holding you back? For example, deep down, do you want to be a doctor, but you've told yourself you are going to get a nursing degree because you think it's easier? Make notes of anything about your current goals that you feel is impacted by your limiting beliefs.

Once you have that list, I want you to make a new list of goals – and when you write it, I want you to completely banish those limiting beliefs from your goal-making process. Every time you write down a goal, revisit your list of limiting beliefs and rewrite the goal until it is as big as it needs to be. Don't worry about what you think you can or can't do, or what you think is realistic. This exercise is not about being realistic; it's about aiming for the sky.

I'm not suggesting that you give over your life to something that is truly not achievable, such as sprouting a pair of wings and flying – but it is important to be ambitious here.

Once you have your list of goals, the next step is to break each one down into achievable mini-goals. Let's use weight loss as an example again. If you want to lose one hundred pounds, your goal might look like this:

Goal: Lose 100 pounds

Daily goal: Keep track of food intake, limit sugar, exercise 30 minutes

Weekly goal: Weigh in once a week, aim for two pounds of weight loss per week

Monthly goal: Take body measurements, try one new exercise.

Six-month goal: Learn how to cook one new healthy recipe a week, increase daily exercise by 25 mins, buy smaller clothes.

One-year goal: Reach goal weight, celebrate.

You get the idea. It is important to break down each goal into more easily achievable sections. If you are just thinking about your end goal – losing 100 pounds – you might feel as if it's impossible. But when you break it down like this, you give yourself a better chance of success. You're telling yourself that it is possible.

Read over your list of goals, and compare it to your old list. I think you'll be as astonished as I was when I first did this exercise. I couldn't believe how much I'd been limiting myself!

DAY 3 – THINK POSITIVELY

Now that you have your list of limiting beliefs and your new list of goals, it's time to dig deeper into something I mentioned earlier: self-talk. Simply identifying new and more ambitious goals is not enough. To achieve those goals, you have to truly believe that you can. While writing down your limiting beliefs is a great first step, it will require a little more effort to rid yourself of them.

What Is Self-Talk?

We talked before about self-talk, but let's go into a bit more detail. We all have internal monologues. Self-talk is the endless stream of chatter that runs through your head every day. It consists mostly of opinions and evaluations of the things you do.

An example of negative self-talk might involve a situation at work. Let's say you have a big project due. You work very hard on it, and you're feeling pretty good about it when you turn it in. However, your boss spots a mistake and calls you on it. A person whose self-talk is mostly negative might say things to himself such as:

- I'm so stupid; I completely messed that up!
- It figures I made a mistake; now I'll probably get fired.
- I can't do anything right.

Pretty harsh, right? You can see why self-talk like that might have a huge impact on the way you think about yourself and what it's possible for you to achieve.

Now let's look at what some positive self-talk might look like in the same situation:

- Wow, I'll have to be more careful next time. Still, I worked hard, and I think my boss knows that.
- Everyone makes mistakes.

- I'm going to learn from that mistake.

The person who engages in positive self-talk is far more likely to rebound quickly from that mistake, and to be successful going forward.

You Are What You Think Exercise

Today's exercise is about taking your negative self-talk and turning it around. You've heard the saying, "You are what you eat." This lesson is about realizing that you are what you think. The great news is, it is possible to change the way you think about yourself with a little effort.

To start, I want you to take the list of limiting beliefs that you made earlier in the week. On a new sheet of paper, write new, non-limiting beliefs for yourself. Let's imagine this was your list of limiting beliefs:

1. I'm not smart enough because I don't have a college degree.
2. I can't dance, I look like a fool whenever I try.
3. I mustn't rock the boat at work. I should just accept things the way they are.
4. Other people are so much more graceful than I am.
5. I don't have the will-power to lose weight.

Those are very negative statements, and looking at them like this, it's easy to see why they might hold you back. A person who truly believed these things about herself would find it difficult to move past her self-talk and achieve her goals.

Now, let's take a look at how the person who had these limiting beliefs might rephrase them in a more positive and affirming way:

1. I might not have a college degree, but I've learned a lot in life, and I have more common sense than most people do.
2. I'm not Ginger Rogers, but I have so much fun when I go dancing that I don't care how I look.
3. Things at work are extremely tough right now, and I'm going to see what I can do to make them better.

4. Sometimes I feel clumsy, but maybe if I try some new physical activities, I would feel more in control of my body.

5. Losing weight won't be easy, but I want to do it and I know I can.

You can see why it would be much easier to maintain a positive frame of mind and achieve your goals if your self-talk looks more like the second example, and less like the first.

Sit down and write your new beliefs out. The thing I told myself when I was doing this is that I should write my new beliefs as if I were talking to a friend, someone I cared about. I would never say to a friend, "You're not smart enough because you don't have a college degree." Why on earth would I choose to talk to myself that way?

Once you have them written, read them over. These are important because you are going to use them to change the way you think about yourself. From now on, I want you to carry these new beliefs with you. As you move through your day, pay careful attention to the monologue inside your head. Whenever you catch yourself repeating one of your limiting beliefs, stop and pull out that piece of paper. Read your new belief. Say it out loud to yourself if you can.

As you become more conscious of your limiting beliefs, you may also identify new ones. If that happens, write them down, and then re-word them in a more positive way.

It may also be helpful to keep track of how many times per day you repeat each limiting belief to yourself. Chances are, some will be in your thoughts more frequently than others. Make note of the ones that are the biggest problem. Going forward, you can use your re-worded versions of those particular limiting beliefs as a mantra or affirmation.

The idea of this exercise is to begin training your brain to think in a new way. That might sound silly, but it's backed up by science. Neurologists now know that our brains are highly malleable and that it is possible to carve new neural pathways if we try. In a way, it's emotional learning.

When we learn a new language, we carve new pathways, too. Overcoming limiting beliefs is about learning a new emotional language.

DAY 4 – MAKING EXCUSES

We all make excuses sometimes because we all make mistakes. Not all excuses are harmful. If you are late getting to work because your bus broke down, it is legitimate to say to your boss, "I'm so sorry I was late. The bus had a flat tire." If your bus gets you to work punctually 99% of the time, your boss will most likely accept your excuse and you can get on with your day.

This chapter is not about that kind of excuse. Instead, it's about the excuses we make to ourselves to justify poor performance, limited goals, or lowered expectations.

You might have noticed that some of the limiting beliefs listed in the previous chapter included built-in excuses:

- I'm not smart enough because I don't have a college degree.
- I can't dance, I look like a fool whenever I try.
- I don't have the willpower to lose weight. (This whole statement is an excuse!)

You can see, looking at these, that none of these excuses are particularly helpful. To the contrary, they are harmful and can get in the way of the person who uses them. Let's take a closer look at excuse-making and the harm it does.

The Danger of Making Excuses

As we get started, it might be helpful to understand why we make excuses. Here are some of the most common reasons:

1. Fear of failure. It is human nature to have a fear of failing when we attempt something. Fear can lead us to make pre-emptive excuses, such as "I probably won't be able to finish this run because it's so hot today."

2. Defensiveness. We all have an instinct toward self-protection. When we make a mistake or fail to achieve a goal, we might be tempted to blame someone else for our failure, or to blame some circumstance beyond our control.

3. Lowering expectations. People who fear failure sometimes try to lower the expectations they have for themselves, or the expectations other people have for them. When you lower expectations, other people may have a rosier view of a poor outcome than they would otherwise.

The problem with making excuses like these is that it's a way of giving yourself permission not to try as hard. It is a form of self-sabotage. For example, someone who's working on a deadline might engage in distracting behavior, such as spending time on Facebook or listening to loud music. The scary thing about this kind of self-sabotage is that often, you won't even realize you're doing it. Very few people consciously think, "I'm going to mess this up on purpose." It's not that easy to identify, which is why you will need to pay very close attention to your self-talk to root out the excuses you are using in your life.

Eliminate Excuses Exercise

As you probably anticipate, today's exercise is about identifying the excuses you are using to justify failure and lack of effort. These are directly tied to your limiting beliefs. For example, I always told myself that I was not artistic because I could not draw in a lifelike way. When I finally let go of that limiting belief, I started taking art classes and found that I have more creative potential than I ever realized.

Start by looking at your original list of limiting beliefs. Take a new sheet of paper, and write down every excuse that appears on your list. After that, look at any statements that did not include an obvious excuse, and look for hidden excuses. Let's look at one of the statements from earlier:

"Other people are so much more graceful than I am."

There is no obvious excuse here, but if you read between the lines, you might be able to find one. For example, maybe the person who wrote this line is using it as an excuse to justify the fact that he's careless with other people's belongings. If he's just not graceful, then he can't be blamed for the fact that he broke that mug, or his neighbor's lawnmower, or whatever. You will need to dig deep to identify all of the excuses you use.

Now that you have a list of excuses, I want you to look at it side by side with your list of goals. Each one of these excuses is something that has the potential to get in the way of your new goals. If you haven't already numbered your list of goals, do it now. Then next to each excuse, I want you to write the number of the goal that you think might be affected by it.

The purpose of doing that is to help you understand the specific things that might hold you back from reaching your goals. If you know that your lack of a college degree might serve as an excuse to prevent you from asking for a promotion or applying for a new job, you can figure out ways to work around it. For example, it might be helpful to write a skills list that focuses on things you know how to do instead of on your educational background. Doing this can help to boost your confidence, because it puts your attention on the things you do have, instead of on those you don't.

I encourage you to spend some time on this exercise. If you want to get at the root of what's holding you back, you need to be willing to examine yourself deeply. When you have finished writing, read over all four of your lists – your original list of limiting beliefs, your rewritten list of positive beliefs, your list of goals, and your list of excuses. Take a minute to pat yourself on the back for all the hard work you've done.

DAY 5 – RAISING YOUR STANDARDS

One of the main things to remember about both limiting expectations and excuses is that they serve to lower your standards. When you tell yourself you can't get a promotion, you are setting a very low standard for yourself. When you don't expect great things from yourself, it is impossible to achieve great things. It's time to raise the bar.

The Importance of Setting Standards

Having standards for yourself matters. People have different kinds of standards for different situations. For example, ethical standards dictate the way we behave in moral terms. They are what keep us from doing things like cheating and stealing. Many ethical standards are societal standards. For example, we have laws against driving over the speed limit. Laws like this are intended to protect us. We need them.

The same is true of the standards we set for ourselves. We need to have them because they help us to define who we are, and what we are capable of doing. Standards become a problem when we set them too low, but they can also be a problem when they are too high. In general, you want to shoot for standards that are high but not ridiculous. If you expect perfection, you are setting yourself up for failure just as much as you would be if you expected to do the bare minimum.

As a rule, most of your standards should be objective ones, meaning they should be easy to quantify. For example, if you are trying to lose weight you might say, "I expect that I will not eat foods that are high in sugar." That is a clear standard. If you eat a candy bar, you will know you have not met the standard you set for yourself.

It is also fine to have some subjective standards. Standards like these tend to emphasize your effort rather than concrete actions:

1. I expect that I will try as hard as I can
2. I expect that I will think about the food I eat before I eat it
3. I expect that I will be successful

All three of these are subjective. Only you know whether you have tried as hard as you can or whether you thought about it before you ate that cookie and success means different things to different people. If you choose some subjective standards, you will need to make sure you clearly define what they mean to you.

Let Go of Failure

One important element of setting standards for yourself is to stop looking at mistakes as failures. Having high expectations for yourself doesn't mean that you have to be crushed every time you make a mistake. In fact, the opposite is true.

One way to change the way you think about mistakes is to surround yourself with people who are more skilled than you are at a particular thing. That might sound counterintuitive but stick with me. To truly get rid of your limiting beliefs, you need to stop looking at mistakes as failures and start looking at them as learning opportunities. One of the best ways to do that is to spend time with people who are more skilled, accomplished, or educated than you are. Ask them questions when something doesn't go the way you expected it to, or when you don't understand.

When we let ourselves get set in a particular way of thinking, it gets harder to change. The best way to keep your brain active and flexible is to continue challenging it. People have a tendency to get mired down in their limiting beliefs – the more they cling to them, they harder it is to let go. The opposite is true too, though. When you let go of those beliefs and embrace learning, you greatly increase the chances that you will be able to reach your goals.

Setting Standards Exercise

Today's exercise is simply to set standards for yourself. Before you start, read over everything you've written up until now, so it's fresh in your head. Then – keeping your goals and your new, positive self-talk in mind, write down what you expect of yourself. It's important to do this in stages. For example, you might start with a list that looks like this:

- I expect that I will never eat anything that is unhealthy for me
- I expect that I will save some money from every paycheck
- I expect that I will treat people with kindness and respect
- I expect that I will keep learning new things

Those are mostly good – and mostly realistic. However, that first one is a bit problematic because it sets an unreasonably high expectation. Saying that you will never eat anything that's unhealthy for you seems like a lot to ask. Take a look at your list, and rewrite anything that seems too severe. The goal here, after all, is to push yourself to excel without setting yourself up for failure. Once you have rewritten it, this standard might say "I expect that I will make an effort to eat healthy foods, and eat unhealthy foods sparingly."

Once you have a list of standards that feels right to you, read the whole thing over and try to internalize them. Don't memorize them, but let them take root in your brain. Read them over a few times if you have to. When you're trying to learn something new, it can be especially helpful to read it over right before going to bed because your brain will continue to work on it as you sleep.

- At this point, you're almost through the week, and I hope you are starting to feel the effects of what we're doing. Next, we'll talk about turning the things we've talked about into actions.

DAY 6 – THE POWER OF MOMENTUM

All of the work you have done so far has been leading to this point. When you started the week, you had not yet identified your limiting beliefs, but they were affecting you every day. Even if you were not consciously aware of them, they were playing a role in the things you decided to do, and those you decided not to do. They affected the goals you set for yourself, as well as affecting the way you worked to achieve those goals. They convinced you to hold yourself to either too low a standard, or to unreasonably high standards.

The lists you have made are going to be your roadmap going forward. They are going to help you let go of your limiting beliefs for good and step forward into a brighter and happier future.

The Importance of Action

You have done quite a bit of thinking about your limiting beliefs. In the end, though, thinking is not going to change your life – not without action. It's natural to be feeling a little apprehensive at this point. You're working on making some big changes to your life, and you're headed into unknown territory. It would be strange if you weren't a little scared.

There is a difference between apprehension and inertia. If you let your fears get in the way of taking action to achieve the new goals you've laid out for yourself, then really all you're doing is giving in to the same old limiting beliefs. With that in mind, let's talk about why it is so important to take the words on your lists, and turn them into actions:

1. **Taking action overcomes resistance**. As I said earlier, it is completely normal to feel some resistance to the idea of moving forward. However, if you don't do it, you run the risk of becoming entrenched in the same thinking that got you stuck.

Remember that you don't have to take a huge action to start with. Nobody's suggesting that you need to climb Mt. Everest on your first day. What you do need to do, though, is to take a step or two in the direction of your goal.

2. **Actions turn into momentum**. Once you start taking a few steps, you will find that it is easy to settle into the swing of doing new things. Think of it this way. When you climb on the treadmill at the gym, the beginning is always brutal, isn't it? Your legs burn, and you feel like giving up. But the more you keep at it, the better you feel. You've got momentum, and having that makes it much easier to keep pushing ahead.

3. **Actions reinforce beliefs**. When you take one of your new, non-limiting beliefs about yourself and put it into practice, you are reinforcing that belief in a big way. You are telling your brain, "This is real. This is the way things are going to be from now on. Get with the program." And the amazing thing about your brain is that it will get with the program. It will follow where you take it.

4. **Actions get results**. Why would you want to spend so much time breaking down your goals into achievable steps if you weren't going to act on them? After all, you know you are never going to achieve a new goal if you don't take action. In other words, if you do not act, you are guaranteeing yourself the worst possible outcome you could get if you did act. Whereas if you do act, you have a good chance of getting the best possible outcome.

Taking action is the only way you are going to stop your limiting beliefs for good, so let's talk about how to do that.

Generate Momentum Exercise

Today's exercise is about taking the lists you've made of your beliefs, goals, expectations, and standards and putting them into practice. The idea here is to give yourself a boost, to reaffirm the things you have been thinking about, and to take action on them. Now, it might seem a little intimidating, and that is understandable. Let me tell you how I made this task easier for myself.

1. Get a planner or calendar, and use it to map out the actions you are going to take. If you don't want to buy something, just print out some blank monthly calendars online and put them in a looseleaf binder.

2. If you have multiple goals you want to work toward, try using different colored pens to track them. You can do the same thing for standards, although those are less like daily tasks, and more like reminders of how you want to behave.

3. Start small. When you are making big changes in your life, it is important not to overdo it. Start by simply planning out your first week. Write mini-goals in for each day. For example, you might write in:
   a. Get to work early
   b. Get started on new project
   c. Go to gym after work
   d. Spend quality time with kids

4. Make sure to include several goals for tomorrow, since that's the last day of the week you've spent learning how to overcome your limiting beliefs.

5. When you have your week planned out, read it over. Then take out your list of limiting beliefs, and try to identify which goals you think are going to be the most challenging for you. If you know that the "I can't lose weight because I have no willpower" limiting belief is going to rear its head on the days you go to the gym, you can prepare yourself for it. On those days, write your non-limiting belief based on the same topic on the margins of your planner or calendar. When you look at your calendar, make sure to read the affirmation. It will help you stick to your goals.

6. Follow the plan you've laid out for yourself. Do the very best you can to achieve your weekly goals. If you miss a day at the gym, or if something else doesn't go the way you planned, be mindful of your self-talk and make sure to stay positive.

The wonderful thing about taking action like this is that, once you start, you will be amazed by how much easier it is for you to feel optimistic about your goals. Action begets optimism. It makes you feel accomplished and competent in a way that thinking alone cannot.

You have come such a long way, and we are almost done with the week. Tomorrow's lesson is about taking stock and looking ahead – two things that I hope will make you proud of what you have accomplished.

DAY 7 – REFLECTION ON THE WEEK

Congratulations – you are now at the final day of the week. Today, you have two main tasks. The first is to head into the day with your calendar or planner and pursue the goals you wrote down yesterday. The second is to reflect on the past week and make a plan to move forward. Let's talk about each task briefly.

Pursuing Daily Goals

Your first assignment today is to do everything you can to meet the goals you wrote down on your calendar. You should probably go into the day expecting some roadblocks. After all, things rarely go exactly the way we plan them. Don't let yourself get sidetracked. Pay special attention to your self-talk, and refer to your list of positive affirmations as often as you need to.

When I first got to the point of having well-planned daily goals, I could not believe how great I felt at the end of the day. I'm not going to tell you that there weren't times I struggled – of course there were. But the feeling of accomplishment I had when I got to the end of my list and checked off that last goal was amazing. It was the best I'd felt in years, and that's not an exaggeration.

It may be helpful to sit down at the beginning of the day and schedule time for certain goals. If you're planning to go to the gym, for example, pick a time and write it on your calendar as if it were a date. It can also be helpful to write reminders for yourself. You might not need a reminder to eat lunch, but writing "Eat a healthy lunch" can help keep you on track.

I recommend making a big deal out of crossing each task of your list. Make a big checkmark next to each thing, or cross it out with a flourish. Your accomplishments deserve to be celebrated.

Reflecting on the Week

Your final task is to reflect on the week that has just passed. One thing I like to do is to write myself a letter. You started the week by writing a list of the things you say to yourself. Why not end it by writing a kind and encouraging letter to yourself, reaffirming everything that you have learned? When you read the letter, you will be surprised to see how different the tone is from how you started the week. At first you were hypercritical of yourself, unkind and judgmental and impatient. By taking the time and effort to examine the way you talk to yourself, you have learned a whole new language in terms of what you believe you can accomplish.

Writing a letter to yourself can be a good exercise to revisit periodically. When you find yourself being negative or unkind to yourself, write those negative thoughts down – and then write a rebuttal as if you were writing to a friend. It is such a powerful exercise, and it's one I use all the time. It teaches you how important it is to be compassionate toward yourself. It will help you rewrite your self-talk, but it will also make you kinder and more compassionate toward other people because you will have a much better idea of what their inner struggles might be.

Let's Reflect on Day 1:

It is very important what you tell yourself because is where you constitute your beliefs. By now you should've gotten rid of some of your old beliefs and replaced them with positive ones. If you're still having trouble, practice the exercise daily until you have at least three beliefs changed.

Let's Reflect on Day 2:

Goals are important when striving for something and it helps you stay aligned with them and stay focused on achieving the desired result without being inflicted. If you're having issues with this exercise of thinking positively about your goals, then focus on only one and actually take actionable steps to achieve them. That will make your mind believe that it's doable with results to back those theories up. Once you do that your limitations should start to fade.

Let's Reflect on Day 3:

Think about what your mind subconsciously associates with your list of goals, is it positive/ negative? If it was negative by now it should have shifted. If not, mentally embody your goal and visualize yourself in that position, that leaves a positive effect on the brain and it'll start to correlate positively with your goal.

Let's Reflect on Day 4:

Making excuses to yourself is a very detrimental limiting factor and you've probably already trained your mind to think of one every time something gets tough, this is a protection mechanism and is human nature, but you can condition yourself to stop those thinking patterns whenever things get difficult, In the exercise you should've already recognized your excuses with every goal on your list. You cannot achieve any of them with a negative attitude so work briskly on it until it's altered. This may not come easily to you but it's in the practice.

Let's Reflect on Day 5:

What do you expect of yourself? Do you have any expectations? Expectations help push you to achieving your desired result and without it, your goal will be just a wish. Talk to yourself about the standards that you set for yourself and internalize it.

Let's Reflect on Day 6:

To achieve momentum you'll need to plan ahead and take small actionable steps every day in order to gain it. For example, maybe you'll decide to get up for work early or make a fixed daily routine of taking your pet out for a walk. This will discipline yourself and make it easier and more manageable to achieve your goals as you'll be in a controlled positive mindset.

SUMMARY

This book has been written with the aim of helping you eliminate your limiting beliefs that were either installed in you from an early age or through choices and failures. When you understand how to break free from thoughts that only limit you, that do nothing but stop you from moving forward, you will start achieving the unimaginable.

Positive and forward thinking are key to achieving your desires, as it's looking back especially on bad situations that holds you back. Reclaim your hopes and ambitions to lead a positive and fulfilled life.

Thank you so much for reading. I hope you find the information here — and the exercises provided — to be as helpful as I have found them to be. I promise you, if you work your way through these exercises and take the time to reflect, you will notice profound changes in your life. Instead of being hindered by limiting beliefs, you will find ways to get in touch with your limitless potential.

Good luck. Not that you need it!

Ruth

OTHER BOOKS BY RUTH LOGAN

Healing - 7 Ways To Heal Your Body In 7 Days (With Only Your Mind)

Gratitude - 7 Simple Steps To Becoming More Grateful In 7 Days

Printed in Great Britain
by Amazon